CONTENTS

A VAST INDUSTRY	3
PRODUCING THIS BOOK	3
PRINTERS AT WORK	4
A variety of processes	
A variety of jobs	
A variety of companies	
PUBLISHERS AT WORK	5
Publishing books	
Publishing magazines	
A SKILLED INDUSTRY	6
A CHANGING INDUSTRY	6
SOME OF THE PRINTERS	7
Creative director	
Full-colour planner	
Scanner operator	
Carton designer	
Trainee machine printer - YTS	
Machine printer - "first minder"	
Screen printer - ex YTS	
Senior printer	
Apprentice print finisher	
SOME OF THE PUBLISHERS	16
Owner of a desktop publishing business	
Magazine art editor	
Senior staff writer	
Editorial manager	
QUALIFICATIONS IN PUBLISHING	20
QUALIFICATIONS IN PRINTING	20
Training skilled printers	
Training printing technicians	
Training printing managers	
WHAT NEXT?	21
Some addresses for printing courses	
Other useful addresses	
Further reading	

EXAMINATION CHANGES

England and Wales
In places in this book you may find references to GCE O levels and CSEs. These have been replaced by GCSE qualifications.

One-year intermediate AS examinations were introduced in the Summer of 1989. They are designed to supplement A levels and offer students a broader choice of subject areas to study.

Scotland
The SCE O grades are being replaced gradually with Standard (S) grades. Schools have a choice of O grade or S grade for a transitional period.

EQUAL OPPORTUNITIES
All the opportunities mentioned in this book are open to all suitably qualified people, whether male or female and regardless of racial origin.

FOREWORD

More than 320,000 people currently work in the printing and publishing industries. Here, they enjoy an environment which offers creativity, challenge and fun, as well as the normal requirements of job satisfaction and security.

The pace of technical change - on a par with the computing and electronics industries - has transformed printing into a hi-tech industry, using some of the most efficient and advanced equipment in the world. Customers' expectations for greater use of colour, innovation and design, together with higher levels of service and productivity, continue to set further exciting demands.

The business world, too, is changing. In 1992, Britain will become part of a single European Market, where there will be free and open exchange with the Dutch, Germans, Italians and all our other continental counterparts. Japan and America continue to play their part on this keenly contested stage.

The printing and publishing industries relish the challenge. We welcome new trainees who wish to join in. Working in the industry is fun and there are many job opportunities.

This publication seeks to introduce the industry and the employment areas open to you. We know you will find it of interest.

COLIN STANLEY
Director General of the British Printing Industries Federation

Working in Printing Publishing

A VAST INDUSTRY

You are looking at just one product from a vast industry. Wherever you are there must be many other products of that same industry all around you: other books and magazines, stationery, boxes, posters, stamps, labels and even wallpaper and fabrics.

Printing is a large industry, with over 200,000 employees working in a variety of companies throughout the country. It's one of our "top-ten" manufacturing sectors, and also one of the highest-paid. Publishing is a smaller industry, with 20,000 people publishing books and another 20,000 publishing magazines. Add all the people who work in the newspaper industry and in reprographics - that's using photocopying equipment - and it becomes an even larger industry.

PRODUCING THIS BOOK

Printers and publishers work very closely together. Here are just a few of the people who were involved in producing this book.

PUBLISHERS

The **EDITOR** chose the title and contacted a writer.

The **WRITER** did the research, wrote the book and provided the photographs. The typescript was sent back to the editor.

The **EDITOR** checked through the typescript, chose which photographs to include and sent the work to a designer.

The **DESIGNER** looked at the words and photographs, then created the layout of each page.

The **TYPESETTER** typed the words as they were to look on each finished page. Galley proofs of each page were sent back to the designer.

The **DESIGNER** put the sections of words and photographs together, and sent sheets of camera ready artwork back to the editor.

The **EDITOR** looked at these final designs before sending them off to the printer.

The **MARKETING** department advertised the book so that people would order copies.

The **CUSTOMER SERVICES** department took the order.

The **WAREHOUSE AND DESPATCH** department sent the booklets to your building...

PRINTERS

The **ACCOUNT EXECUTIVE** looked after the job as it went through all the printing stages.

The **PLANNER** laid out all the page artwork to fit into the size of a printing plate.

The **PLATEMAKER** made the printing plate with a very large "process" camera.

The **MACHINE PRINTER** fixed the plate onto the printing press, made some test copies and then printed all the pages.

The **PRINT FINISHER** put the cover and pages together, then stapled and trimmed the finished books.

The **DESPATCH** staff packed the finished books and sent them back to the publisher.

AND YOU ARE READING IT!

PRINTERS AT WORK

A VARIETY OF PROCESSES

Printing is simply the process of transferring ink onto paper, or perhaps onto card or plastic, or even onto metal or glass. This can be done in different ways, and with different types of equipment. Some of these processes have unusual names like flexography and gravure printing. The main method used today is lithography, and there are even different versions of that process.

The process used for each job depends on the type of work being done, and what the ink is being printed onto. For printing onto paper, the "offset-litho" process is probably the most widely used type of equipment, or press. Many of these presses use the very latest electronics technology, but other printing processes, such as screen printing, use very traditional methods.

The screen printing process is one of the easiest to understand. It is a type of stencilling, with ink simply rubbed through a screen stencil onto card or cloth, or onto more unusual surfaces such as curved plastic and glass bottles. Although some screen presses may be modern and automatic, others are still completely hand operated.

The different printing presses come in all shapes and sizes. Some printing companies use large factory buildings, with presses that nearly fill the area from floor to ceiling. These can operate at speeds of up to 50,000 sheets an hour. Other printing companies may use small offset presses that take up just a few square metres of floor space. Companies usually specialise in one method of printing.

A VARIETY OF JOBS

People working in smaller firms may do a variety of jobs during a day. Those working in larger companies often specialise in one of the great variety of skilled jobs in this industry.

New orders usually start in the administration section of a printing company. Here there are:

- **sales representatives**, who travel to see customers;
- **production controllers**, who talk to the customers, and look after the order as it passes through the various stages of production;
- **estimators**, who work out how much the order will cost to print;
- **buyers**, who buy all the materials needed for each job; and
- **managers**, who control the operation of the company.

Before the printing presses can be switched on the order must pass into the origination section of the company. Here there are:

- **keyboard operators**, who work at a computer keyboard. They set the size and style of typeface to be used, then type in the text;
- **proof readers**, who check through the text and make any changes;
- **make-up compositors**, who lay out the text with the illustrations to fit the designs for the pages. In some companies this is all done on a computer screen;
- **camera operators**, who photograph the pages;
- **planners**, who put sets of four, eight, 16 or 32 pages together according to the size of the printing plate; and
- **platemakers**, who use a very large type of camera to produce the plates, ready for the printing presses.

The finished plates - usually four different ones for full-colour printing - are taken through to the machine printing section of the company. Here there are:

- **machine printers**, who fix the plates onto the presses, load the ink and paper, make the correct settings for colour and speed, take proof copies for checking and then print the work. Large presses are operated by teams of up to four machine printers.

The printed sheets are then either taken to the finishing department of the company, or sent to a separate print-finishing company. Here there are:

- **print finishers**, who operate machines to cut, crease, fold, stitch and bind together anything from books to boxes; and
- **packers and despatch staff**, who sort, pack and wrap the finished products ready for the customer.

A VARIETY OF COMPANIES

There are many differences in the type of work done by different companies. Some may take orders for a few hundred sheets of headed notepaper, but there are others that can handle orders for over a million copies of a 96 page full-colour catalogue.

Some printing firms give a wide range of services, but the very large companies often specialise in one type of work. These specialist companies may concentrate on anything from books to boxes or banknotes. Some companies also specialise in one stage of the process by giving an origination, machine printing or print finishing service to other companies.

PUBLISHERS AT WORK

Publishing companies - or 'houses' - vary in size in the same way as the printing companies. Some are large companies with many branches. Others are very small firms with just a few staff. Many of the apparently small publishing houses are now owned by a few very large publishing organisations with world-wide interests.

PUBLISHING BOOKS

Like any other type of manufacturing, the book publishing industry can be split into design, production, marketing and sales departments. The difference is that books are not usually manufactured in the publishing houses. Most publishers use the services of specialist printing companies, but a few of the large houses have their own printing establishments.

New books start in the editorial department of a publishing house as typed or word-processed manuscripts. In small publishing houses all the editorial work may be done by one person. In large houses there may be:

- **editors**, who read through the enormous number of manuscripts sent in by hopeful authors. They have to decide what is suitable for publication, and what to reject;
- **commissioning editors**, who know the type of non-fiction book they want to publish. They contact suitable writers and commission them to produce the manuscript of the book. They may also make some changes before the book passes to the production stage;
- **desk editors**, who look after the new book as it is being published; and
- **copy editors**, who check through the proof copy of the book to correct any mistakes before printing.

The edited manuscript is sent to the production department where it must be changed into the style of a printed book. The typeface to be used has to be chosen, and photographs or drawings may be needed. Once these have been chosen the words and pictures can be put together by deciding what the layout of each page will be. The book is then ready for printing.

The work of the publishing house continues after the book has been printed. The sales and marketing department must advertise the book, and sell as many copies as possible. They may also deal with export orders. Sales representatives visit bookshops, exhibitions and major buyers.

Small publishing houses often use freelance staff. They are paid for each job that they do, and often work for other publishers as well. Freelance or full-time production staff may include:

- **designers**, who create the layout of each page;
- **illustrators**, who produce any drawings or diagrams that are needed;
- **picture researchers**, who find the photographs that are needed;
- **indexers**, who make the indexes for detailed non-fiction books; and
- **proof readers**, who do the work of the copy editor.

PUBLISHING MAGAZINES

With over 5,000 titles in print, magazine and periodical publishing is one of the main parts of the industry. The well known titles that are seen at the newsagents are the consumer magazines. The numbers of people who buy these magazines make up the 'circulation figures' which can be very high for popular titles.

Many more trade magazines and periodicals for different businesses are published, but their circulation figures are usually much lower. They are often sold by subscription, but many are provided free.

Each title has its own publisher, but many companies publish more than one title. As with book publishing, many of the magazine publishing companies are controlled by a few large multinational organisations.

The work starts in the editorial department. Here there are:

- **production editors**, who decide exactly what will go into each issue, and look after all the stages of production;
- **staff writers**, who write any articles that are needed;
- **sub-editors**, who alter and check the articles; and
- **art editors**, who design the layout of the magazine.

Most magazines need the help of advertisers, who pay for the space they use. The advertising department must sell the space reserved for advertisements in each issue. They also need to keep records of how many copies are sold. The distribution department must move each issue from the printers to wherever it is sold.

A SKILLED INDUSTRY

Printing is a highly-skilled industry. Those working in the origination section need to be able to work carefully, and concentrate for long periods on very detailed work. Keyboard operators and proof readers must be able to spell accurately, and understand grammar and punctuation. Make-up compositors will need design skills, as their work controls the final look of the product. Mechanical skills are important for machine printers and print finishers. Good colour vision is important for most of the jobs in the industry.

Publishing houses need people with specialist skills that range from design to distribution. Editors and their writers have very creative jobs, but they need just as many business and financial skills to make their company successful. Many people working in magazine publishing have a background in journalism. Lots of people are attracted to this type of work, but the first job can be difficult to find. Starting salaries can be low and the working hours are often long.

A CHANGING INDUSTRY

Publishers still choose words and pictures, and printers still put them onto paper, but the way they do their work is changing very quickly. There are computer systems to process the words, set the type and design the pages. Other computer systems can control the printing presses. Printed words and pictures can be sent around the world almost instantly using facsimile (facs) machines. Printing and publishing are high-tech industries.

One example of this change is development of **desktop publishing.** Programs can be used with small office microcomputers to set type, process photographs and diagrams, and make up pages. The equipment often includes another electronic development - a laser printer - that will make a high quality copy of the finished work. This can either be photocopied, or used to make a plate for a printing press.

These desktop publishing systems are being introduced to offices, schools, colleges and some small publishing houses. Companies such as the high street 'instant' printing shops often offer a desktop publishing service to their customers.

SOME OF THE PRINTERS

Kath Fairburn is the creative director for Whitehead and Wood Ltd - a large print, packaging and design company. She designs brochures and advertising material for major companies such as engineering firms, textile manufacturers, and retailers. The company then produces the items that Kath has designed.

'When I was still at school I was determined to make a career in graphics. I had to take a different job at first but I eventually found a job vacancy and started as a studio assistant on the staff of a local newspaper. The studio produced the artwork for different advertisements.

'A few years ago it was far more difficult for women to make a start in this type of work, and it was three years before I was allowed to start an apprenticeship. That apprenticeship then went on for the next five years - but it was well worth the long wait.

'There were no day-release courses for me to try. It was five years of purely industrial on-the-job training during which I learned a great number of graphic skills. I am sure that being part of a busy graphics studio is still one of the best ways of learning the many skills of this job.

'I moved from that studio to an advertising agency where I became their art director. After a short period in an American advertising agency, also as an art director, I came back to Britain and worked for a company that produced a range of promotional material. While I was with them I helped to design The Times "Portfolio" game, and many of the scratch cards that are given away. From that job the next career move brought me to my present company.

'My official day is from 9 am to 5 pm, but in this type of work the length of the day depends on how much work has to be finished off that day - so I usually work for much longer than my official hours.

'The company is in Lancashire and weekly trips to see customers in London and elsewhere mean days that start at about 5.30 am. As creative director I lead a team of three full-time artists, one 'board mechanic' who tests out the designs for the card boxes, a studio manager, a typesetter and a proof reader.

'When I am not visiting customers, my days are varied. I usually start by checking through the proof copies of jobs that arrive in the post each day, then I talk to my studio manager about the various jobs being done at the time.

'I spend a great deal of time dealing with business on the telephone, but not enough time dealing with all the paperwork. I often have to take that home with me. There are sales representatives to see, and many visits to the printing room and other departments of the company. Customers usually ask us to take the various designs to them before printing work can start.

'Another part of my work is to deal with any photographs that are being included in a job. I have to choose and book a photographer, choose and book a model, book a make-up artist and stylist and arrange for any "props" that are needed for the shots - and all to be ready for the same time. A good publicity photograph also needs a good setting, and finding those is another part of my job. I try to make a note of good locations as I travel around the country for the company.

'I have had a range of jobs in the graphics part of the printing and publishing industry, and I think my work has become more and more interesting each time. I enjoy all the parts of my present job, from the stage when customers talk over an idea, and give us a "brief" to design and print something for them, to the stage when the finished product leaves the printing presses.

'Probably the most rewarding stage of all is still the presentation. That's when I take a display of finished designs along to customers for them to see before the printing can start. When they tell me that they are just what they were hoping for, and that we can go ahead and print, I know I made the right career choice.'

Wendy Finn works as a full-colour planner at Spa Graphics Limited. This is one of the many smaller companies that specialise in origination work. She turns designs for pages into printing plates, ready to be sent to a machine printing company.

'I had all sorts of ideas for my career while I was still at school. By chance, my first job was with a company that put diagrams and other information onto microfilm. I was taught how to do all the film processing. I chose the photographic side of the printing industry as my next career move by becoming a studio assistant for a design company.

'Design studios produce artwork for what each finished page will look like after printing. I worked in the repro section of the company, where we made photographic copies of the artwork. Using a special type of camera, called a process camera, I had to copy all the artwork onto large sheets of film. These films were then used to make up the finished printing plates.

'I didn't train through an apprenticeship scheme. I was given on-the-job training, with experienced planners teaching me all the skills while I was actually doing the work. I also had to learn about all the new processes as they were being introduced. I worked in the planning section of a few printing companies before taking my present job as a full-colour planner.

'I work closely with our scanner operators, such as Jerry Rowden. He will explain how coloured photographs have to be scanned to give the three colour separations, plus black, on film. Jerry makes the separations and I have to work out exactly how they will fit together as I plan the printing plates.

'A new job comes to me from the designer. It is often a page of artwork with some colour photographs and sections of text. I photograph all the pages onto large sheets of film, and work out where all the colour separations are needed. When these come back from the scanner I can fit them onto the films in exactly the right places.

'Most of the printing plates here are large enough to take eight, or even 16 pages at a time. One of the last jobs is to fit the films of those pages together in the right pattern. I have to plan how they should be laid out so that, as the sheets come off the printing press, they can be folded to give 16 pages in the right order.

'Once I have planned the layout of all the films on one printing plate, that plate can be made. This is another photographic process, and it is done with automatic equipment. The finished plates are the end product for this company. They are carefully packed up and sent off to the customer. The customer will give them to the printing company that they choose. We do not have our own printing presses. When I want to see what a complicated plate will look like after printing I have a "proof copy" made from it instead.

'I do most of my work standing at a light table - that's a table with a white plastic top and lights underneath. It shines light through the films to help me see exactly what I am doing. My normal working shift lasts from about 8.30 am to 3.30 pm, but the company has a great deal of work these days. Each job needs to be finished by a set time. I am given a certain number of jobs to do each day, and that can mean doing overtime to finish some jobs off.

'I need to use similar skills all the time, but the work is always interesting because each new job that comes in is very different. Some of the jobs can be difficult, such as when there are many colour separations to match up|- or register - perfectly.

'Few other women worked in this industry when I started. Things are changing now as more girls are choosing a career in origination. I am not certain how my own career will develop from here. I may go into the management side of the industry, or I may decide to start my own origination business. Colour planning is the sort of job with many opportunities for skilled employees, and there are many growing companies to choose from.'

Jerry Rowden prepares photographs and other illustrations for the printing process. After a full apprenticeship as a camera operator he now uses some of the latest computerised electronic scanning and page make-up equipment. He works for Spa Graphics Limited.

'I started out in the industry a few years ago. It was at the time when apprenticeships lasted for a full five years, and I trained as a camera operator. It seemed to be a good way of combining my interests in art and commercial photography. I took day-release courses at a local college during my training, and qualified with a City and Guilds certificate in photo-litho work.

'Although I had trained for lithographic- or litho- printing, I worked for some time as a camera operator in firms that used gravure printing presses. These are the very large presses that are used for long print runs of perhaps well over a million copies each time. My job was in the origination side of the industry. That meant I did the photographic work involved in making the printing plates.

'The printing industry has changed a great deal in recent years. Many printers have moved to different companies, and learned new printing skills. I moved from the gravure company to a firm using litho printing methods. Litho printing has become more and more important in recent years.

'I still work in the origination side of the industry, by preparing colour photographs for printing. The equipment I use will give you just one example of how this industry has changed, and is still changing. I now operate an electronic scanner to prepare all the coloured artwork and photographs. It's a very advanced, and very expensive, piece of equipment which has a computer controlled laser in it.

'Colour printing cannot be done by using a lot of different coloured inks on the same printing plate at the same time. Anything, such as a colour photograph, that is being printed in full colour has to be split up into all the types of yellow, all the types of cyan (blue), all the types of magenta (red) and all the blacks. These are called colour separations. A printing plate is made for each of the separations. The four plates are fixed to different parts of the press, and the paper passes by each plate in turn, gradually building up the colour.

'It's the scanner that makes those four separations from the original photograph or artwork. Once I have fixed the photograph onto a perspex drum, and set the focus, the really skilled part of the job starts. I have to make very accurate measurements to make sure the balance of colour and the exposure will be perfect. It takes many years of experience, even after the apprenticeship years are over, to do the job well. It also takes perfect colour vision of course.

'I work a system of double day shifts. One week I work early days, from 6.15 am to 1 pm and the next week I work late days, from 1 pm to 8 pm. We are very busy so there is often some overtime to do as well. Once the scanner has warmed up, and the chemicals are prepared, I am ready to start operating the scanner for the rest of the shift. I work on my feet most of that time.

'The scanner makes the separations by a photographic process. They are put onto film in another part of the machine. The films are processed automatically, and then sent over to our planning department to be turned into the printing plates.

'Even this high-tech process is changing now. We have just bought an electronic page make-up system to add to the scanner. Whatever the laser in the scanner measures can be sent to the page make-up computer, instead of being developed onto film. It looks just like a computer VDU next to the scanner, but it shows a very high-quality version of the original picture.

'By looking at the screen and using the controls, I can make changes to the picture, or take out scratches and other marks. Once the changes are finished the information goes back to the scanner to make the films in the usual way. It's just an extra stage in the scanning process for customers who want the very highest quality work, or who need to have pictures changed in some way.

'Origination work is technical and skilled. It is a part of the industry where new technology is leading to new processes and new skills all the time. The work done in this part of the industry is the key to any printing job. High quality separations and plates mean high quality printing at the end of the day. Learning all the necessary skills, and then being able to use them well, gives you what so many people call job satisfaction.'

Packaging is an important part of the complete printing industry. Its products are all the card boxes and cartons used to protect and display products. Jackie Collins started as an apprentice, and is now a carton designer for Vibixa Limited. She designs and makes samples of cartons before they are printed in bulk.

'Technical drawing was one of my favourite subjects at school. When I left, I applied to this company, and I was offered a technical apprenticeship. It seemed a very good way of using my technical drawing. The apprenticeship lasted four years, and was linked to a course at the London College of Printing.

'I spent the first year working full time for the company to introduce me to the job, and then went on block release. This meant going to college for a few weeks at a time, and I spent a total of 20 weeks at college for each of the next three years.

'The college course was a mixture of practical carton making and printing theory - there's more to making a box than you might imagine. When I wasn't at the college I worked for short periods in many different departments of the company. This taught me about all the other stages in packaging production, and how our company operated.

'By the end of the apprenticeship I had a City and Guilds Certificate in Carton and Box Making, as well as four years' experience of doing the job. When the apprenticeship period finished I carried on working the usual pattern of 6 am to 1.30 pm shifts one week, and 1.30 pm to 9 pm shifts the next week.

'The method of designing and making sample cartons has changed tremendously in the few years that I have been doing the job. The skill of designing a carton is creating a shape, including all the folds, flaps and tucks, that can be cut out in one piece. It also involves fitting as many of those shapes as possible onto the large sheets of card that are fed into the printing presses.

'Everything has to be done very accurately, or else the cartons will not make up properly. I used to draw the designs, then crease and cut out the card samples by hand. I now use some of the most up-to-date computer equipment to design and make those samples.

'We put the new CAD/CAM computer system in about three years ago. CAD/CAM means "computer aided design/computer aided manufacture". In other words we use the computer to design, and then draw and cut out all the samples. The computer looks like any other microcomputer: as I build up the design I can see it on the screen. 'Instead of having a small printer by the side of the computer, it is linked to a large plotter. This has a moving arm that can draw the design, and then crease and cut the large sheet of card. I went on a short course to help me use the equipment, and I have learned how to program the computer for each design I create.

'Many different food-making companies ask us to design and print cartons for them. My job has to be done before the factory can start printing any order. By using all the equipment I can make a sample of what any carton will look like, as well as an accurate drawing. This is sent to our estimating department. They work out how much the design will cost to print. My sample, and the cost of the job, can then be sent to the customer. If the customer decides to go ahead, the work is sent back to me for the next stage. Getting a design to work out, and then please the customer, is always rewarding.

'I fit as many of the individual designs as possible into a much larger design, as we print many cartons on each sheet. I use the plotter to draw the large design onto clear film, and that is used for making the printing plates. The artwork comes from another department.

'One final design is plotted out, but this time on a large sheet of wood which goes to our die-making workshops. Thin metal strips are slotted into the wood along each line where a cut or a crease will be. These also go down to the printing machines. As the sheets are printed they are pressed against these dies, and the cartons are cut and creased. Die-making is another very skilled job in the packaging industry.

'There are seven of us in the sample and die-making department, and we all work as a team. I am the only woman in this department, and I was the only girl in a class of 25 when I was at college. Printing used to be a male-dominated industry, but things are changing now. More women are coming into the industry - particularly the graphic and design areas of work.'

Simon Arrowsmith has only recently started his career in printing. He is training to be a machine printer through the Youth Training Scheme, and works for Cooper Clegg Ltd - a major printing company producing magazines and many other publications.

'When I was still at school I knew I wanted to do a job that involved working with some form of machinery. I visited local colleges to look at their different courses, and I also contacted companies to ask about vacancies. I decided to take the offer made by this company of a full two-year training in machine printing.

'Although I am still in my second year of training, through the Youth Training Scheme, I am already a full employee of the company, which means I earn more than the basic YTS allowance. If all goes well with my training I will have qualifications in machine printing at the end of the two years.

'Being a trainee means that I am based at the company for four days each week, when I work as a full member of a team of machine printers. I spend the fifth day studying at a nearby technical college. It is a college with a large printing department. The facilities are good and they run many different printing courses.

'My usual hours when I am at the company are 8 am to 4 pm with a lunch break. The day at college is much longer: I start at 9 am but often have to work through to about 7 pm.

'I am studying for the City and Guilds Certificate in Printing (523). The course covers all parts of the printing industry, but I am specialising in machine printing. It is a very practical course, with plenty of projects to do. Some of the recent topics that I have been studying include planning and plate-making as well as setting-up the various machines.

'The course also includes a little physics and chemistry, computer studies, design studies and communications. I meet my YTS tutor regularly to discuss how I am getting on with the work at college.

At the end of each year there are some written exams to take.

'When I am back at work I am part of a team working on a very large automatic four-colour web offset press. The paper is fed in from a large roll that weighs over a tonne. The press is much larger and faster than anything we have at college, where we have to feed in sheets of paper by hand. A normal team has just four people: a 'first minder' who is in charge of the team, and has responsibility for the quality of the work; a 'second minder'; and two assistants to help keep the machines running. I am training to become a second minder on the press.

'My jobs already include fixing the printing plates onto the machine and carefully setting and checking the dials that control the mix of colours. Once the press has started I help to check that the machine is running smoothly. Some of my other jobs are helping to stack all the finished work as it comes off the press, changing reels of paper and barrels of ink, and taking copies from the machine so that they can be checked.

'There are many things to do just to get one job through the press. We may have as many as five or six different printing jobs to set up in a day and that means there is certainly plenty for me to do when I am at work. All the different jobs mean that I am working on my feet most of the time.

'There is plenty to enjoy in this job. One of the most satisfying things is when I have set the controls on the machine so that the colours being printed exactly match the colour of the proof copy. We can print in what seems to be a never ending variety of colours. Being able to create the exact colour wanted by the customer is very important.

'I also enjoy looking at the finished products. When we print the pages of a book we print many pages at once on the same sheet. Before they leave the press they are folded to make them ready for binding into the finished book.

' ' Many printing firms send their work to a different company - a print finisher - to be fixed together and trimmed to shape. That means it's difficult to ever see the finished product. We have our own print finishing company next door so I can easily see all the finished items that I have helped to print.

'There are many skills to learn to be able to run a large press at full speed. The work can be hard at time and the hours long in a busy company, but I am already looking forward to the end of my training. My ambition is to become a second minder on a similar machine, and with luck I should progress to first minder before too long.'

Carl Bretherton works for Cooper Clegg Ltd. as an experienced machine printer and shift leader. He is in charge of some of the largest and fastest presses that are available.

'People choose printing as a career for different reasons. For me it was a family tradition going right back to my grandfather. My father is a printing works manager. They had told me a great deal about the work so when I was 16 I decided to leave school and start a printing apprenticeship.

'My apprenticeship was organised by the BPIF (British Printing Industries Federation), and it lasted four years. During that time I had both day-release and block-release from my firm to study for a City and Guilds Certificate in Machine Printing.

'I spent 18 months of my apprenticeship learning the first stages in the printing process - planning and plate making. I used to plan the best way of fitting pages onto large printing plates, and then make the plates that the machine printers fixed onto the presses. After that I went into the machine room as a trainee, and gradually worked my way up to learn all the machine printing processes.

'I worked as a second minder for a while and was then given the job of first minder - the person who is in charge of the team of four printers who operate the press. I am now also a shift leader, which means that I have to supervise other teams as well as lead my own team during a shift.

'The company I work for is large. We have just moved into new buildings, and have put in the very latest equipment. Some of our web offset presses are large enough to hold plates that will print 16 pages at a time, and then fold them into sections.

'We can run the large presses at a rate of anything up to 50,000 copies an hour, both day and night. The presses may be very large but it isn't particularly heavy work. We have hoists to help with the really heavy job of changing the rolls of paper.

'When a new job arrives I start by setting the press up for the new printing plates, paper and ink. Before the machinery can start to print at full speed I have to check that the colour is exactly right. We print some copies to look at, and when I am sure the colour is satisfactory I will sign the proof copy.

'The next job is to set the part of the press that folds the sheet into the final pages, then it is time to start printing. As the press is running I supervise the work of my second minder and keep a check on production. We do most of the routine maintenance on the equipment as it is running. Sometimes customers call in to talk about progress on their orders.

'Because there are so many orders at present I work twelve-hour day or night shifts. Some weeks I work from 6 am to 6 pm and other weeks from 6 pm to 6 am. The company always guarantees to pay us for a minimum 371/2 hour week. There are higher rates of pay on the night shift, and all extra hours are paid at the overtime rate.

'I enjoy working in our small team and, like many other printers, I find looking at the finished product coming off the press very satisfying. We print a great number of glossy brochures for customers such as holiday companies. You have probably read something that has been printed on our machine. Our brochures are sometimes even shown in television advertisements.

'My advice to anyone thinking about a career in printing is simply to go and see for yourself. If you can arrange a visit to a printing company it is probably the best way to understand what happens in the industry; we have work experience links with a nearby secondary school. I hope my own career will lead me to the next stage in the industry as a printing works manager.'

Dennis Dawkins has trained as a screen printer. He works for Priestley Studios Limited, a company that produces a range of products such as shop counter displays, stands, signs and posters. Screen printing is a process that can be used to print onto paper, card, board, plastic, glass, fabric and even wood.

'I always enjoyed art lessons when I was at school. When the time came to start choosing my career I decided to try to use my interest in art in some way. Although my first idea was to work as a signwriter, I had also thought about a career in the printing industry.

'As it happened, the first job I was offered was as a part-time temporary worker with my present company. After a short while they gave me the chance to stay on with them, and qualify as a screen printer through the Youth Training Scheme.

'Screen printing - or silk screen printing as many people still call it because the screens were once made from silk - is a straight-forward type of printing that is a little like stencilling. The stencil is made to match the shape to be printed, and it is copied onto a very fine mesh screen.

'Ink is scraped over the screen; it passes through the gaps in the stencil and onto the paper below. Screen printing gives one colour at a time - a new screen is needed to print each colour - so it can be a very slow process.

'My training was a course at the printing department of the local technical college for one full day each week. At the end of two years I had a City and Guilds Certificate in Screen Process Printing. I am now in my first year after finishing the course.

'My days at college were very full as we started at 9 am but didn't finish until after 7 pm. However, the course was practical and enjoyable. There were a number of screen printing or other projects that we could choose from for ourselves, and I learned a number of skills whilst I was there.

'Back at work my days are usually a little shorter. I operate the printing equipment between about 8 am and 4 pm, then there is the important job of cleaning the machine each day before leaving. Fridays mean an early finish, but as we are usually busy there is often some overtime available for Friday afternoon and Saturday.

'Many of the items that I print are used for point-of-sale advertising. They may be small display stands made from thick card, and used on shop counters or in window displays.

'My work starts with carefully fixing the screen onto the machine. After loading the first sheet of card I pour the ink onto the screen. The machine spreads the ink, and it passes through the gaps in the stencil to print onto the card. I then take the freshly printed card out, lay it on a rack to dry, and I am ready for the next sheet.

'Most jobs need more than one colour. Another screen is made with a stencil of the area for the second colour. After about half an hour the first colour will have dried. The cards need to be very carefully lined up with the registration marks before they can go through the machine for a second or, perhaps, a third time.

'We have our own preparation department with full-time screen stretchers, who stretch the fabric over the frames, and full-time stencil makers, who use a photographic process to stencil the shape onto the screen. Like many other printing companies we also have our finishing department where the printed shapes are cut out, folded and made ready for the customer to make up. I suppose all printers must enjoy seeing their finished work, and it is the same for me. I can see many of the display stands I have printed each time I go to the shops.

'I enjoy screen printing and I haven't thought too much about my future yet. With a few more years' experience my next job could be as a foreman in the printing department, supervising other screen printers. From there it may be possible to move into a management job, or perhaps into some form of design work.'

Shelly Neal is a senior printer in a busy Kall Kwik high street printing centre - one of the many 'quick print' companies that have opened in high streets throughout the country in recent years.

'My interest in printing started with my first job after leaving school. I worked as an office junior at a building society, and helped in a very small printing department for some of the time. We produced all the forms that were needed by the society. As the department grew I began to work on the printing machines all day - it's been my career ever since.

'From the building society I went on to work for three other printing companies, using their small offset printing presses. Although I haven't had a formal apprenticeship in the industry, each change of job has given me more on-the-job training and a great deal of printing experience.

'I now work as a senior printer for this high street centre. Like many similar businesses it's a franchise company. This means the owners set up their own businesses but buy the right to use a well known name, and have the shop fitted out and equipped to look like the other printing centres in the country with that name. We work in a shop, in a busy city high street.

'Like most of the other high street printing shops, the company has expanded in recent years to provide a full range of printing services. We are a full printing company in minature, and can produce glossy covered booklets in full colour, as well as all the usual business and private stationery. We even employ two artists so customers can have their work designed for them.

'I am meant to work from 8.30 am to 5.30 pm, with a break of an hour for lunch. With so many customers these days I usually start an hour or so earlier, and often work much later - and working means being on my feet for most of the day.

'My first job for the day is to cut and pack all the orders I printed the day before, so that they are ready for the customers to collect. I spend the rest of the day printing a great variety of small and large orders such as letterheads, message pads, envelopes, cards, forms, and booklet pages and covers. Each job is different: one customer may want just a hundred cards and another may want 20,000 forms.

'Before I can print anything I need to make the printing plates, either from the design that our artists have made, or from something the customer has brought in for us to copy exactly. I use our large process camera, placing the finished artwork under a glass sheet, and setting the controls. The printing plate is made from a type of paper. It is developed automatically and clipped onto the press.

'If a customer asks for a special colour, I have to mix the ink before starting the machine. When it's a small job this setting up often takes longer than the actual printing. Once I have printed the right number of copies I take the plate off, clean the machine, and it's time for the next plate to be made.

'The small offset printing presses that we use are fairly straightforward to operate, but I do most of the close register colour printing now. That means that if an area of one colour has to be printed right up to another area of colour, with no white gap and no overlap showing, I have to work very carefully indeed - that's what we call the close register work. I think this type of printing is probably the most enjoyable part of my job, but it's also the most difficult.

'The big offset presses in the large printing companies print all the different colours in one operation. Each time I do a job in more than one colour I have to clean the machine, change the ink and run the paper through again. Getting a really complicated colour printing job just right for a customer is a challenge that I really enjoy.

'I have been working in this industry now for nearly ten years. In all that time I have found the small firms the most enjoyable to work in, and they are usually very friendly places - even if things can be a little hectic at times. I like the work I do now but one day I may move into the administration side of the industry. I hope it will be in this size and type of company.'

Jonathan Stark is training to be a print finisher with Whitehead and Wood - a major print, packaging and design company. He is in the second year of the British Printing Industry Federation (BPIF) Apprenticeship Scheme.

'I had chosen a career in print finishing before I left school. I started my apprenticeship by going to college full time for the first term. Since then I have been to college for just one day each week, and worked for the company for the other four days.

'When I finish my college course later this year I hope to have a City and Guilds Certificate in Print Finishing. I will still be an apprentice for another two years, but I will be working full-time at the company.

'College days start at 9 am and last until 6.30 pm, but my normal working day lasts from about 8.30 am to 4.30 pm, with two ten-minute breaks and half an hour for lunch. Fridays mean a much earlier start of 6 am and much earlier finish of 1.30 pm. We are a very busy company, which means plenty of overtime is available.

'The work of a print finisher starts where the work of the machine printer finishes. The company prints many things, including a great deal of packaging and cartons. Our printing presses are all sheet fed, which means they print onto single sheets rather than on huge rolls of paper.

'When the presses are used to print cartons and other boxes I learn how to operate the card folding and glueing machines. The glueing machine applies areas of glue, and makes a carton that can be folded up and fixed together easily. All I have to do is load the sheets and take them off: that may sound easy, but setting the machine accurately is quite a skill. It would be impossible for us to make up each box or carton, as we wouldn't have the room to store them all. They are folded flat when they leave the finishing department, but they can quickly be made into cartons by the customer.

'When the same presses are used to print the pages and covers of booklets, I learn to use the folding, trimming and stitching machines. When we are making booklets, we print 16 pages on one sheet. I use a folding machine to fold the pages in the right way, and to fold the covers. The trimming machine, or guillotine, is probably the easiest to use. It is very large, and can trim hundreds of sheets at a time. All I have to do is set the machine for where I want the cut, load the sheets and square them up, operate the blade, and stack the cut sheets.

'The last machine I use will put all the 16 page sections of a booklet together, add the cover, stitch them together, and trim three edges. The word stitching dates back to the days when book sections were sewn together: we use staples now but still call this stitching.

'My training started by watching a supervisor using each of the machines. After a while I helped, and then gradually took over myself. The work certainly isn't just machine minding. We will often set up many different jobs in a day, and each one can be very different. All the precision machines have to be set very accurately to do the work correctly. There is still a great deal to learn before my apprenticeship finishes.

'I think it is the variety that helps to make the work enjoyable. I could have chosen an apprenticeship as a machine printer, but I am glad I stuck to my first idea of working in the finishing end of the industry.

'As an apprentice, I am already a full employee of the company, and I am looking forward to staying on and working as a qualified finisher. Before long I hope I can reach the next grade of supervisor, and perhaps have my own stitching, folding or cutting department to look after.'

SOME OF THE PUBLISHERS

Hussein Fatemian owns his own desktop publishing company. He also provides a word processing and typesetting service for many customers in his area.

'My experience in the printing and publishing industry goes back to the days when I had my own printing company in Tehran. It was a large company with many staff, and we produced a range of brochures and magazines using traditional letterpress equipment.

'Now, with just one assistant, I use the very latest microcomputer programs and a range of very advanced electronic equipment to do work in minutes that would once have taken hours.

'Desktop publishing is a part of the industry that has developed in just a few years. When I started the business about eight years ago I thought I was setting up a word processing company. I provided a word processing service, for local companies which wanted to produce long reports and booklets, and sold word processing equipment.

'I introduced a desktop publishing service about four years ago. It became popular with customers who wanted to have pictures and diagrams with the words. It also became popular with people who wanted to have their reports printed, as the finished pages looked more interesting than those which had been simply word processed. I continued with the word processing, but desktop publishing became a more and more important part of the business.

'My customers are small and large companies, and local authorities. They usually want me to produce technical manuals and booklets, but I also do some advertising leaflets and posters.

'The original copy, or manuscript, is usually typed. The first stage is to re-type it, using a word processing program to set the words out in different ways - I can make important words stand out by making them darker or larger.

'Some of my customers give me their copy already typed and saved on a computer disc, which saves a great deal of time. On the other hand, if customers give me a manuscript that is very well presented, I can simply pass it through a machine called a scanner which copies it, and puts the words on the screen. Once all the words are stored on the computer I use another program to check for spelling mistakes.

'Photographs and diagrams are also passed through the scanner, and stored in the computer memory using a different program. Another program is used to create diagrams and charts for customers who cannot provide their own.

'The desktop publishing program uses all the words and illustrations created by the other programs. Working one page at a time, I use the computer screen to move blocks of words around to where they look most effective. The size of diagrams or photographs can be altered to fit the spaces available.

'When a page is complete I print out a copy using a laser printer. This works at a rate of up to eight pages a minute, for text only. With photographs or diagrams it takes longer. The results look just like printed pages, but the laser printer is too slow and far too expensive to use for printing many copies of each page.

'When I am working on a booklet or long manual I use other companies to turn the pages into printing plates, print all the copies and bind them into the finished products.

'I try to work the standard hours of 9 am to 5 pm, but having your own business doesn't always work out like that. If there is a great deal of work due quickly I will work much longer hours. I can even take some work home with me using a portable microcomputer.

'Many companies are beginning to buy their own desktop publishing equipment. However, having the right equipment is one thing, but being able to use it is another.

'I am sure there will be plenty of work, and career prospects, for many years to come for all the small organisations that provide a printing or publishing service for other companies.'

Pam Mayers has worked as a freelance layout artist and is now the art editor for "Just Seventeen" magazine. She is responsible for the style of each page of the publication.

'When I was still at school my only firm career idea was to do 'something in the arts'. I left school at 16 and went on a two-year art foundation course at a local college. The course gave me the chance to try many different skills, and I began to work out my career ideas a little more clearly.

'I chose to work in design, and applied for a place on a three-year degree course at a college of art. As the course progressed I developed a variety of design skills, and did a practical project during the final year. A part of that project involved designing the layout of some brochures.

'Designers often work on a freelance basis. They are self-employed and do jobs for many different people; instead of a regular wage, they are paid for each piece of work they do. That's the way I started out - as a freelance layout-artist for a small design company. I worked in their studios designing the layout of brochures and letterheads. This was a good start, but it didn't give me the freedom to develop my own style.

'I knew that what I really wanted was to work on magazine layouts. I also knew that to get a job such as that I would have to build up a folder of my work, and telephone magazine offices to ask if I could meet them. That's how I first met the staff of "Just Seventeen". They looked through my folder and offered me a week of freelance design work. Luckily the week turned out to last for a year.

'When the company that owned "Just Seventeen" launched the new "Looks" magazine, I was offered the security of my first full-time job. I was a junior designer, which meant designing the layout of words and pictures on the pages.

'My next steps were to senior designer and eventually art editor. Just three years after leaving college I returned to 'Just Seventeen' as the art editor - and I have been enjoying that job for the past three years.

'Each new issue starts as a flat plan, or drawing, of how the completed issue will fit together. My work involves checking the progress on the plan and making sure there are no missing articles or photographs. I give designers different pages to work on each day and study their designs from the previous day. I still manage to do some of the design work myself, particularly if there is a special feature I want to work on.

'As the magazine gradually takes shape I pass all the completed pages, with the artwork and photographs, to my production editor. He has the job of taking the page layouts on to the printing stage. This is a weekly magazine but we work on three issues at a time. As one issue is being prepared for the production editor I am working on the layout of the next issue, and writers are working on articles for the following issue.

'My working day starts somewhere between 9.30 and 10 am. The official 6 pm finish often extends to 7 pm. I work at my own desk but, with the rest of the production team sharing the same large office, it is usually an up-and-down day. There are production deadlines on a weekly magazine to meet, and three issues to keep going all the time.

'I can't really have any slack days. This makes the job very demanding, but at the same time very exciting. It is also very rewarding to see ideas that I have had developed right through to the finished publication.

'If you are interested in designing and layout work for a career, the magazines you like reading are a good starting point. One of the reasons why I enjoy working on "Just Seventeen" is because I still enjoy reading it. Study the layout of the pages used in the magazines that you like: why do you like them? Look at other magazines with different layouts: how are those layouts different? Start sketching your own page layouts and keep all your drawings. My final piece of advice is to go to art college and enjoy the course.

'Although magazines are published in towns and cities throughout the country, most of those I would like to work for are published here in London, or in Dundee. I am not certain where my next career move will take me. It may be as an editor of a magazine in the "young" market, or perhaps as an editor of a totally different type of publication.'

Andrew Fleming is the senior staff writer for 'Just Seventeen' magazine. He meets the top pop musicians, and writes about them for the publication.

'When I was 16 I was always reading magazines and thinking what a great job it would be to eventually work for one. I stayed on at school to take SCE Highers before moving south to take a higher national diploma course at the London College of Printing. Although it was a business studies course the main subject was journalism.

'I was already writing magazine articles at this stage, and the course gave me more writing opportunities through brief periods of work experience with various publishers. Like most writers wanting something to show future employers, I kept copies of everything that I had written and used them when I went job hunting.

'My first job was on 'Just Seventeen' as the junior writer. In less than a year, as more senior writers left, I was promoted to become a permanent staff writer, and then the senior staff writer. I am responsible to the editor of the magazine and to the assistant editor.

'My job is to find out all I can about the top pop musicians, interview them and create articles for each issue of the magazine. I write about the people and about their latest recordings.

'The working day varies with what there is to be done, but I never start much before 10 am. Once I have checked the post and looked through the papers I spend most of the day on the telephone. I speak to press officers from record companies, and many other people in the business to find out everything that's happening.

'As I have to write my articles three weeks before the magazine is published, the dates of new record releases are very important to me. I also have to arrange interviews with the current stars themselves. Most of the top stars are difficult to track down, but they have press officers who can make all the arrangements.

'Once I have fixed the time and date of an interview I'm on the telephone again to book a photographer and make-up artist. Lunch breaks often mean just a sandwich at my desk while I am working, but some days I am taken out to lunch by people from the record companies.

'If I spend all day on the telephone, how do I manage to write the articles? I usually start my writing at about 6 pm and then work on through the evening, perhaps as late as midnight. When I interview someone I use a pocket-sized cassette recorder. During the evening I listen to the tape and make a transcript - a written copy - of every word that was said. By then I am ready to start writing the article using a word processor.

'All the time I am writing I use everything I know about the market and all the people that make up the pop scene. In pop writing it isn't necessarily being a brilliant writer that gets you noticed. When the articles are finished I pass them to the editor, and she sends them on to the designer who can then start work on the layout of that page.

'There is so much to enjoy in my job. There are interviews to do at least twice a week, and they mean meeting all the top stars in the pop world. When I am not writing during the evening there are all the concerts and parties to go to. There are also the tense moments when I listen to the charts on Sundays. I might have interviewed a band four weeks earlier and written an article about the success of their next release - three or four weeks later. My job is not only to meet the stars and write about them, but also to get my predictions right. The long hours that I work may be unusual, but my work is really my two hobbies - writing and pop music. I really think it is a privilege to be able to do this job.

'At the moment I am working in two different industries - pop music and publishing. My career could eventually take me in either direction. I enjoy my work so much that I haven't thought about any future job plans. The next step should probably be to move into management as a magazine editor or assistant editor, but that would be a move away from the pop writing, and I don't want to do that.

'When it comes to advising future magazine writers all I can do is repeat what was said to me by all my friends when I was still at school. When I told them I would like to be a pop writer they used to tell me to 'be a realist' and that I would never make it. But I did!'

Merle Thompson is the editorial manager for Stanley Thornes (Publishers) Limited. This is a large educational publishing company, which produces a wide range of school and college textbooks.

'I always knew I wanted to work with books in some way as a career. After staying on at school to take a range of GCE A levels, I went to university and studied for a degree in history. My first job was with a small publishing company where I worked as one of the copy editors, checking through pages and making any changes that were needed.

'When I left that company I decided to change career for a while, and I became a history teacher, though I didn't forget my interest in publishing. After teaching I returned to publishing, and it has been my career ever since. My teaching experience was important because my return was to a firm of educational publishers. As one of the desk editors, I was responsible for some of the school textbooks that the firm was publishing. I looked after new books - or titles - in subjects such as history and English.

'After desk editing my next job with the company was as a commissioning editor. This meant making decisions about the new titles that we were going to publish and contacting authors who could do the work. When their writing was finished they would send me the typed manuscript of the book. From that job I eventually moved to become an editorial manager with my present company, just over a year ago.

'As the editorial manager I have a team of twelve editors. Each one looks after the books that we publish in one subject area. I also have a picture researcher to find all the photographs that we need, and a secretarial assistant. Those are all full-time members of the company.

'I have another team of about 20 freelance editors who do a great deal of the work on the new books. They usually work from home, and are paid a fee for each job that they do for us.

'My working days are quite long. They usually last from 8.45 am to 6 pm or even later. My days are also very busy as we are a growing company. We have recently taken over another educational publishing company. There seems to be more and more work coming in all the time.

'I spend much of my time working at my desk, or in meetings with editors and production staff. We have to decide what the finished pages will look like, or what artwork we need from the artist. My work also means that I have to travel from time to time and talk with some of our freelance editors, artists and writers.

'It's difficult to describe a typical working day as much of my time is spent trouble-shooting, or solving problems as they crop up. With 120 new books being published at the moment there can be quite a few problems to solve at times.

'Scheduling new publications is one of my main jobs. I have to work out, in advance, the dates when each stage will be reached. When will the page designs be ready? When will the artwork be ready? Proof copies? Final printed copies? The dates on the schedule are important, but with so many people involved things can be held up at times.

'My work on a new title is finished as soon as the camera-ready copy has been made and thoroughly checked through. This is the final version of the book with each page looking exactly as it will once it has been printed. It is sent to our production department, and from there to the printing company. "Camera ready" means that each page is ready to be photographed by the printer, and printing plates made from the film.

'The production department keeps in contact with the printing company. The finished books are sent back from the printers to our warehousing and despatch department. The promotion department has the job of telling customers about new titles as they are ready.

'Like anyone working in the publishing industry I enjoy seeing the finished books when they come back from the printers. It is always a satisfying part of the job. For me, perhaps the most satisfying part of my work is getting things through on time, and seeing that the whole system is working.'

QUALIFICATIONS IN PUBLISHING

Publishing companies offer a variety of careers, each with different entry qualifications. There are opportunities for school and college leavers, but a university degree is still the usual qualification for careers on the editorial side.

Graduates go into publishing with degrees in a wide range of subjects. Educational and technical publishing companies often recruit graduates with specialist degrees for editorial work.

Companies may provide short in-service training courses, or send employees to specialist training centres. There are also post-graduate courses at a number of colleges and universities.

A few specialist full-time courses in publishing are available for people with GCE A level/SCE H grade certificates, or suitable BTEC qualifications.

These include:

- a degree in publishing, and various diploma courses, at Napier Polytechnic, Edinburgh;
- a modular degree with a publishing option at Oxford Polytechnic;
- various BTEC higher national diploma and certificate courses at the London College of Printing.

The exact entry requirements for these courses vary. Please check the current prospectus for each college.

QUALIFICATIONS IN PRINTING

TRAINING SKILLED PRINTERS

A new training scheme has been introduced for skilled workers coming into the industry as school or college leavers. It is based on an agreement between the British Printing Industries Federation, which is the employers' organisation, and the printing trade unions - NGA and SOGAT. Trainees learn the skills of the industry through a combination of on-the-job training at their printing company, and day- or block-release to college.

College study is based on the new City and Guilds 524 Graphic Communications course. Trainees, and their employers, select the most suitable course, which must last for a minimum of two years, part time. They can select sections of the course dealing with origination, machine printing or print finishing. Trainees working for more specialised printing companies can select a course in bookbinding, graphic design, screen printing, reprographics or even carton and box making.

There are similar training arrangements in Scotland, but the apprenticeship period lasts for a minimum of four years. The various printing courses form part of a SCOTVEC national certificate.

Entry requirements vary from company to company. Employers look for high standards of education, and many require good GCSE/SCE O/S grades in English, mathematics and technical or scientific subjects. The majority of trainees start as school or college leavers, but there are no restrictions on adult entry to the courses.

TRAINING PRINTING TECHNICIANS

The rapid technological changes in the industry have led to an increasing demand for printing technicians. Full-time BTEC national diploma, and part-time BTEC and SCOTVEC national certificate courses are available at a few colleges. Entry qualifications are usually four GCSEs/SCEs O/S at grades A-C/1-3, including English, or a City and Guilds Certificate in Printing.

For students without the necessary entry qualifications, or for people who cannot attend a nearby day-release course, the Open Learning programme from Watford College includes a BTEC national certificate course in printing.

TRAINING PRINTING MANAGERS

A few specialist full-time courses in printing are available for people with GCE A level/SCE H grade certificates, or suitable BTEC/SCOTVEC national certificate or diploma qualifications. These include:

- a degree in printing and packaging technology at Watford College;
- a combined studies degree, including an option in printing technology, at Manchester Polytechnic;
- various full-time or part-time BTEC and SCOTVEC higher national diploma and certificate courses in printing at:
  Glasgow College of Building and Printing
  London College of Printing
  Manchester Polytechnic
  Napier Polytechnic of Edinburgh
  Robert Gordon's Institute of Technology, Aberdeen
  Trent Polytechnic, Nottingham
  Watford College.

The exact entry requirements for all these courses vary. Please check the current prospectus for each college.

WHAT NEXT?

What can you do if you want to find out more about careers in the printing and publishing industry?

- Talk to a careers adviser, such as your school or college careers staff.
- Collect as much information as you can. Many of the organisations in the list of addresses will send you careers information.
- Contact some of the colleges if you are interested in taking a course. They will give you information about both full-time and part-time courses. They may also arrange visits or open days.
- Use the local Yellow Pages to find out how many printing and publishing companies there are in your area.
- Perhaps you can arrange a short period of work experience, or a visit to one of the companies.
- Ask your library to find you some of the books listed at the end of this book.

SOME ADDRESSES FOR PRINTING COURSES

Berkshire College of Art and Design
Kings Road
Reading RG1 4HJ
0734 583501

Brunel Technical College
Ashley Down
Bristol BS7 9BU
0272 241241

Cambridgeshire College of Arts and Technology
East Road
Cambridge CB1 1PT
0223 63271

Castlereagh College of Further Education
Montgomery Road
Belfast BT6 9JD
0232 797144

Glasgow College of Building and Printing
6 North Hanover Street
Glasgow G1 2BP
041 332 9969

Gloucestershire College of Arts and Technology
Brunswick Road
Glouchester GL1 1HS
0452 426602

Kitson College of Technology
Cookridge Street
Leeds LS2 8BL
0532 430381

London College of Printing
Elephant & Castle
London SE1 6SB
01 735 8484

Manchester Polytechnic
Cavendish Street
Manchester M15 6BR
061 228 6171

Matthew Boulton Technical College
Aston Road
Birmingham B6 4BP
021 331 5990

Napier Polytechnic of Edinburgh
Colinton Road
Edinburgh EH10 5TD
031 444 2266

South Fields College of Further Education
Aylestone Road
Leicester LE2 7LW
0533 541818

South Manchester Community College
Barlow Moor Road
West Didsbury
Manchester M20 8PQ
061 434 4821

South Nottinghamshire College of Further Education
Farnborough Road
Clifton
Nottingham NG11 8LU
0602 212347

Watford College
Hempstead Road
Watford WD1 3EZ
0923 57500

OTHER USEFUL ADDRESSES

Book House Training Centre
45 East Hill
Wainscot
London SW18 2QZ
01 874 2718

British Printing Industries Federation
11 Bedford Row
London WC1R 4DX
01 242 6904

Business and Technician Education Council
Central House
Upper Woburn Place
London WC1H 0HH
01 388 3288

City and Guilds of London Institute
76 Portland Place
London W1N 4AA
01 278 2468

Institute of Packaging
Sysonby Lodge
Nottingham Road
Melton Mowbray LE13 0NU
0664 500055

Institute of Printing
8 Lonsdale Gardens
Tunbridge Wells
Kent TN1 1NU
0892 38118

National Graphical Association (1982)
Graphic House
63-67 Bromham Road
Bedford MK40 2AG
0234 51521

Periodical Publishers Association
Imperial House
11-19 Kingsway
London WC2B 6UN
01 379 6268

Publishers Association
19 Bedford Square
London WC1B 3HJ
01 580 6321

Scottish Publishers Association
25A South West Thistle Street Lane
Edinburgh EH2 1EW
031 225 5795

Scottish Vocational Education Council
24 Douglas Street
Glasgow G2 7NQ
041 248 7900

Society of Freelance Editors and Proof Readers
Rosemary Cottage
Fore Street
Weston
Hitchin
Herts SG4 7AS
0462 79577

Society of Indexers
16 Green Road
Birchington
Kent CT7 9JZ
0843 41115

Society of Master Printers of Scotland
48 Palmerston Place
Edinburgh EH12 5DE
031 220 4353

Society of Picture Researchers and Editors
Box 259
London WC1N 3XX
01 404 5011

Society of Young Publishers
12 Dyott Square
London WC1A 1DF
01 836 8911

SOGAT (82)
SOGAT House
274-288 London Road
Hadleigh
Essex SS7 2DE
0702 554111

FURTHER READING

BOOKS

Careers Encyclopedia (articles on printing and publishing),
by Audrey Segal, published by Cassell.

Directory of Further Education,
an annual publication by CRAC.

Directory of Publishing,
an annual publication by Cassell.

Guide to Educational Courses in the Printing Industry,
a free publication from The Institute of Printing.

The Media: Magazines,
by Kim Walden, published by Wayland, 1988.

The Media: Book Publishing,
by Julia Knight, published by Wayland, 1988.

Occupations (articles on printing and publishing),
an annual publication by COIC.

Finding Out About Printing,
by Alan Jamieson and Ivor Power, published by Hobsons, 1989.

Inside Book Publishing,
by Giles N. Clark, published by Blueprint, 1988.

TRADE PUBLICATIONS

If you visit any printing or publishing companies you may be able to look at copies of these magazines:

The Bookseller
Inprint
Litho Week
Print (NGA)
Printing Today
Printing World
Publishing News
Sogat Journal

VIDEOS

Both the British Printing Industries Federation and the National Graphical Association produce up-to-date careers videos. These are normally available from careers centres, or from careers departments in schools or colleges.

THANKYOU

... to all the individuals featured in the book.

... to the following organisations, for all their help and support.

The British Printing Industries Federation
Cooper Clegg Limited
Just Seventeen Magazine
Kall Kwik Printing Centres
Komori Europe Limited
Priestley Studios Limited
Q & S Desktop Publishing
Spa Graphics Limited
Stanley Thornes (Publishers) Limited
Vibixa Limited
Visual Marketing Services
The Department of Printing and Packaging at Watford College
Whitehead and Wood Limited

... and to
Tom Jones-Sandell
Director of the British Printing Industries Federation
(South Western Region)
and
Tony Keeble
Director of Education British Printing Industries Federation